I WONDER WHY

Snakes Shed Their Skin

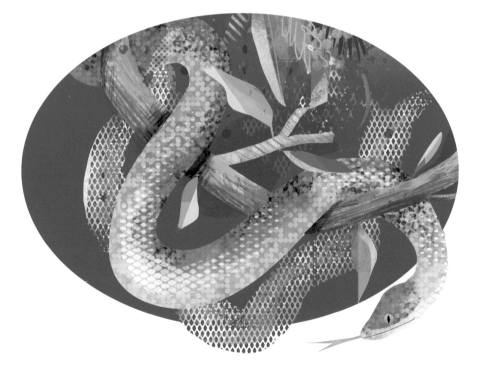

KINGFISHER

LONDON & NEW YORK

KINGFISHER
LONDON & NEW YORK

Copyright © Macmillan Publishers
International Ltd 2011, 2024
Published in the United States by Kingfisher
120 Broadway, New York, NY 10271
Kingfisher is a division of Macmillan
Children's Books, London

ISBN: 978-0-7534-7947-6 (HB)
ISBN: 978-0-7534-7948-3 (PB)

Distributed in the U.S. and Canada by Macmillan,
120 Broadway, New York, NY 10271

EU representative: Macmillan Publishers Ireland
Ltd, 1st Floor, The Liffey Trust Centre,
117-126 Sheriff Street Upper, Dublin 1, D01 YC43

Library of Congress Cataloging-in-Publication
data has been applied for.

Author: Amanda O'Neill
Consultant: Michael Chinery

2024 edition
Editor: Seeta Parmar
Designers: Peter Clayman, Amelia Brooks
Illustrator: Gareth Lucas

Kingfisher books are available for special
promotions and premiums. For details contact:
Special Markets Department, Macmillan, 120
Broadway, New York, NY 10271.

For more information, please visit
www.kingfisherbooks.com.

Printed in China
9 8 7 6 5 4 3 2 1
1TR/1123/WKT/RV/128MA

FSC
www.fsc.org
MIX
Paper | Supporting
responsible forestry
FSC® C116313

CONTENTS

Which animals are reptiles?

Snakes, lizards, crocodiles, and turtles all belong to the same animal group—**reptiles**. All reptiles have a **bony skeleton** and **scaly skin**. Most of them lay eggs, which hatch on land. But some reptiles give birth to their babies.

CROCODILE

TORTOISE

Reptiles are cold-blooded, which means that their body temperature changes with the temperature outside. They have to warm up in the sun to become active. If they get too hot, they move into the shade.

SNAKE

Reptiles live on land and in the sea almost everywhere on Earth. But they don't like the cold, so you won't find them around the North and South poles.

LIZARD

The tuatara of New Zealand looks like a lizard—but it isn't. It has no living relatives on Earth. They all died out more than 200 million years ago!

FROG

Are frogs and newts reptiles?

Frogs and newts are not reptiles. Along with toads, they are **amphibians**. They have no scales, and their skin is very thin. They lay their eggs in water, and their young hatch as **tadpoles**. Baby reptiles look just like their parents, only smaller.

TADPOLES

NEWT

Which is the biggest reptile?

The **world's biggest reptile** is the saltwater crocodile of tropical Asia and Australia. This huge beast can grow to more than 23 feet (7m)—as wide as a soccer goal.

The fastest reptile is a North American lizard called the six-lined racerunner. Over short distances, it reaches speeds of 18 miles per hour (29km/h)!

ANACONDA

SALTWATER CROCODILE

Tortoises can be found on all continents except for Australia and Antarctica, and live in many different environments including deserts, grasslands, and forests.

Which reptile lives the longest?

Tortoises can live to a really old age. The oldest one ever known is over **190 years old!** But this might not be a record—there could be even older tortoises in the wild.

The smallest reptile is a tiny chameleon lizard from Madagascar. It measures 0.8 inches (2.2cm) from top to tail.

Which is the biggest snake?

The biggest snake is the anaconda of South America. It grows to more than 33 feet (10m)—that's **as long as a bus**. The reticulated python is another whopper, but although it's as long as the anaconda, it's not as heavy.

Do snakes have good table manners?

Snakes are **not polite** at mealtimes. They don't chew their meals—instead, they swallow them whole! They stretch their mouth over their food until it's all gone. And their jaws and body are so **elastic** that they can eat things much bigger than themselves.

Snakes can bend and twist because their backbone is made up of hundreds of tiny bones all linked together like a chain.

Most snakes are loners, but hundreds of rattlesnakes will snuggle together underground to sleep through the cold winter months.

Why do snakes have teeth and fangs?

As well as having teeth to grip their food, poisonous snakes also have a pair of **fangs**. They use these long teeth to strike their prey and **inject** them with poison, which shoots out of holes at the fangs' tips.

An attacking cobra raises its head and spreads out flaps of skin on its head to form a scary-looking hood.

Vipers have extralong fangs that fold down flat when they're not in use. This is helpful—they wouldn't be able to shut their mouths otherwise!

Why do snakes stare?

Snakes stare because they **can't blink**. And they can't blink because they have no eyelids. Each eye is covered by a see-through scale that protects the eye.

Whose tongue is longer than its tail?

The chameleon's **sticky-tipped tongue** isn't just longer than its tail—it's longer than its whole body! The lizard shoots it out in an instant and reels it back in with a meal.

Why do lizards lose their tails?

Lizards can **snap off their tails** when they're being attacked. The dropped tail wriggles, puzzling the enemy and giving the lizard time to escape. A new tail grows in a few weeks.

Why do geckos lick their eyes?

Most lizards have **eyelids** to wipe their eyes, but the gecko doesn't. Like a snake, it has a scale across each eye. To keep its eyes **moist and squeaky clean**, the gecko licks them, using its long tongue like a handy wipe.

Most lizards are landlubbers. The marine iguana from the Galápagos Islands is the only one that lives in the sea.

Are there dragons on Earth?

The **Komodo dragon** may not have wings or breathe fire, but it is truly awesome. It's the **world's largest lizard**—longer than a car and heavier than a couple of prizefighting boxers. When people first saw one about 100 years ago, they thought they were looking at a **dragon**!

11

Which reptile is a living fortress?

Living inside a shell is like living inside a fortress. At the first sign of **danger**, a tortoise retreats inside the shell's thick walls, blocking the "doors" with its feet and claws. It's well protected from **attack**, and from **heat** and **cold**, too.

A tortoise's damaged shell will slowly heal. A vet can help by patching it with fiberglass, a lightweight material used to build boats.

BEAK

A tortoise could never park its shell and leave it behind. The shell's horny plates are connected to the skeleton underneath.

Do turtles have teeth?

Turtles don't have teeth, but their **horny beaks** have plenty of bite. Alligator snapping turtles are especially fierce. One bite from them and you could lose your toes!

12

A tortoise's shell keeps out most enemies, but eagles and vultures have "cracked" the problem. They drop the poor animals from a great height and smash their shell.

Tortoises live on the land. Turtles have flippers for swimming and live in the sea.

Terrapins are tiny turtles that live in rivers and lakes.

Which turtle breathes through a snorkel?

The spiny soft-shelled turtle spends most of its time **underwater** in rivers and ponds. It doesn't need to come up to the surface to breathe. It pokes its long snout out of the water like a **snorkel** and draws in a noseful of air.

13

Which animal is like a submarine?

An alligator lies so low in the water that it's **hidden like a submarine**. Its eyes, ears, and nostrils all lie on the top of its head so that it can still see, hear, and smell things while most of its body is **underwater**. Other animals don't even know it's there—until it grabs them!

ALLIGATOR

GHARIAL

Gharials belong to the same group as crocodiles and alligators.

Why do crocodiles eat together?

When one crocodile makes a kill, as many as **40 friends** will join in the meal. It might look like a tug of war, but the animals help each other by **tearing off chunks** that are small enough to swallow.

Did you know that crocodiles eat stones? The weight keeps them low in the water so they can hide from their prey.

Crocodiles are fully waterproof! When they dive, special flaps seal off their ears, throat, and nostrils, and extra eyelids act like underwater goggles.

It's easy to tell an alligator from a crocodile. If all the bottom teeth are tucked inside the mouth, it's an alligator. If the fourth bottom tooth sticks out, it's a crocodile.

CROCODILE

PLOVER

What makes a crocodile smile?

A crocodile never smiles, but it looks like it does. It is actually **panting** so that its body heat escapes through its mouth and the animal **cools down**.

Did you know that crocodiles go to the dentist? They open their mouth and let plovers hop inside. These birds pull out pieces of old food and any little insects that they find there.

15

How do lizards move in a hurry?

Some lizards find that they can move much quicker if they run on **two legs** instead of on all fours. When something disturbs a crested water dragon and gives it a fright, it likes to make a speedy getaway. So the lizard stands up, pushes on its powerful back legs, and **hurries off** as fast as its legs will carry it.

How do snakes move without legs?

Snakes manage very well without legs. One of the ways they move is by throwing their body into **zigzags**. By pushing back against stones, they force themselves forward. Many snakes are good swimmers and tree climbers, some burrow underground, and others even glide through the air.

Basilisk lizards can run on water, thanks to flaps of skin on their feet. These create tiny air pockets that keep the lizards afloat while they are running. However, they can only travel short distances before sinking underwater.

How do crocodiles swim without fins?

Crocodiles may not have fins like a fish, but they have **a very powerful tail**. By lashing it from side to side, crocodiles use their tail to **propel them** through the water like an oar. They tuck their legs in very close to their body to make themselves as smooth and as streamlined as possible. That way, they slip along **incredibly fast**.

Which lizard looks both ways at the same time?

A chameleon's eyes **swivel** around and can even move in different directions from each other. This doubles the lizard's chances of spotting **something to eat** and makes it hard for a moth to sneak by without being seen!

Why does a snake flick its tongue?

As a snake's tongue darts in and out, it picks up **scents in the air**. The tongue carries the scents up to a sensitive area in the roof of the mouth, which tastes the air. This area sends messages to the **brain**, telling it whether a mate, a meal, or an enemy is near.

When the cave anole lizard comes out into the sunshine, it closes its eyes and peeps through scales in its lower eyelids. The scales protect its eyes like a pair of sunglasses!

What use is a hole in the head?

If you're a lizard, a hole in the head is very useful—because it's probably an ear! Most lizards have an ear on each side of their head. It's just an open hole leading down to the **eardrum** inside. Reptiles' ears don't stick out from their head like ours do. Snakes' ears are hidden inside their head.

Rattlesnakes and other pit vipers can hunt in total darkness. They can sense the body heat of a nearby animal and strike their prey with amazing accuracy.

Why do some reptiles disguise themselves?

Reptiles use **disguises** to hide themselves. Some of them hide to help them get a good meal. A hidden hunter blends in with the background and won't be seen until it pounces on its prey. Other reptiles hide to **protect themselves**—they don't want to become someone else's lunch! And some reptiles have markings that make them look more dangerous than they really are.

EYELASH VIPER

The eyelash viper of Costa Rica in Central America is bright yellow. It's perfectly hidden among the fruit of the golden palm.

Chameleons are the masters of disguise. They can change their color to match their surroundings—well, almost!

Some turtles have a flat, smooth shell, which looks just like pebbles. The shell helps them to hide on the river bed, keeping a lookout for their prey.

MILK SNAKE

Can you spot the difference?

CORAL SNAKE

The Australian leaf-tailed gecko is almost invisible against a tree trunk. Its speckled skin blends in beautifully with the bark.

The milk snake is completely harmless, but it protects itself from enemies by pretending to be dangerous. It has the same color stripes as the poisonous coral snake. Can you spot the difference?

Crocodiles can be mistaken for logs floating in the river—that is, until they suddenly strike!

Which reptile has a frightful frill?

If you frighten an **Australian frilled lizard**, it will try to frighten you back. It has a frill of skin around its neck that it can open up **like an umbrella**. This makes the lizard look twice its real size. And when it also **stretches** its mouth wide open, it's a pretty terrifying sight!

AUSTRALIAN FRILLED LIZARD

Steer clear of the horned toad from the southwestern United States. It isn't really a toad, it's a lizard, and it can squirt jets of blood—from its eyes! Scary!

Which turtle kicks up a stink?

The **stinkpot turtle** of North America has earned its name! When it feels threatened, it lets out a **yucky smell** that quickly drives away its enemies. And they don't come back!

The stumpy-tailed skink has a stumpy tail that is the same shape as its head. As long as it keeps its mouth shut, its enemies can't tell whether the lizard is coming or going!

Why do some snakes pretend to be dead?

Some snakes face danger by pretending that they're dead. The **European grass snake** rolls on its back and lies perfectly still with its mouth open and its tongue hanging out. The enemy probably won't want dead snake for lunch and will leave it alone. Then the clever snake comes back to life and makes its escape.

EUROPEAN GRASS SNAKE

Which turtle fishes with its tongue?

The alligator snapping turtle has a wriggly pink tip on its tongue that looks **just like a worm**. The turtle lies on the bottom of the lake with **its mouth open**. To any fish, the "worm" looks like a meal. But if the fish swims up hungrily, it's snapped up by the turtle instead!

Which snakes give a deadly hug?

A python could survive on just one meal a year—so long as it's something the size of a young zebra.

Boa constrictors and pythons don't poison their prey. Instead, they **squeeze** it tight until it suffocates to death. They have such a **deadly hug** that they can kill a goat, pig, or deer in less than a minute.

Who enjoys a mouthful of prickles?

Most smaller lizards are meat eaters. They eat only insects or small animals. But the green anole makes sure it gets its vitamins and eats fruit as well!

Like many large lizards, the land iguana of the Galápagos Islands is a **vegetarian**. It likes nothing better than a cactus for **dinner** and can munch on the spines without feeling so much as a **prickle**!

People who live in warm countries are often happy for lizards to share their home. The lizards eat up lots of insect pests.

Which reptile stays in its egg?

Young snakes take their time about hatching. Having broken open its shell, a youngster pokes out its **head to look around**. It may decide to stay safe inside for a day or two longer before it slithers out **to explore**.

Baby reptiles have a special tooth to cut their way out of the egg. It drops off once it's done its job.

Which reptile lays the most eggs?

A **green turtle** lays more than **1,000 eggs in a season**, in holes she has dug on the beach. Then she can be certain at least some of her young will survive. Gulls, crabs, rats, foxes, and fish all feast on the **tiny turtles**. Only one turtle in 1,000 may grow to be an adult.

Which reptile is the most caring mother?

Male or female? The sex of baby crocodiles, turtles, and tortoises is often decided by how warm the eggs have been before they hatch.

Most reptiles leave their eggs or babies to take care of themselves. **Crocodile moms are different**. They guard their nests from hungry birds and other animals, help the babies **hatch out** of their shells, and carry them in their mouth safely down to the water.

Do reptiles have skin like ours?

A reptile's skin is quite **tough and horny**— more like our fingernails than our skin. On snakes and lizards, most of the skin is covered with **small scales** that overlap one another. But crocodiles and turtles have even tougher skin, with **hard plates** instead of scales.

Snakes don't feel slimy. They're dry, cool, and pleasant to touch.

A reptile's scaly skin holds in water and stops the animal from drying out. This is useful if you live in the desert, as many lizards do.

Why do snakes shed their skin?

Like your **old clothes**, a snake's skin wears out and needs to be replaced—often in a bigger size. So from three to seven times a year, the old skin splits open and **peels off**, and—presto!—there's a brand-new skin waiting underneath.

A snake's old skin begins to split at the lips. The snake wriggles out headfirst, turning the skin inside out as it goes. The skin often comes off in one piece, in a perfect snake shape.

Why do some lizards have horns and spikes?

Horns and spikes are a good way of protecting an animal. Like a strong **suit of armor**, they make a lizard look fierce—and they also make a prickly mouthful for any animal that tries to attack.

Why do reptiles need our help?

Many reptiles are in **danger of dying out** forever, because of humans. People hunt them, or destroy the places where they live. Climate change is **another big threat** to their existence.

Sadly, the beautiful skins of many reptiles are still used for leather goods such as wallets, belts, shoes, and bags.

The loggerhead turtle is in danger of extinction. Tourists invade the beaches where it breeds and, out at sea, thousands get tangled up in fishing nets and die.

In the past, so many tortoises and other reptiles were caught to be sold as pets that they became rare. Now, there are laws to stop people from collecting and selling wild animals.

Many endangered reptiles, such as the golden mantella frog, are now being looked after in zoos. In time, their young may be returned to the wild.

American alligators can be found in the Everglades National Park in Florida. Only 20 years ago the animals had nearly disappeared, but—thanks to tough laws— there are plenty of them now.

INDEX

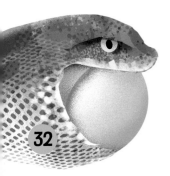